Also by Victoria Chang

POETRY

The Trees Witness Everything
OBIT
Barbie Chang
The Boss
Salvinia Molesta
Circle

NONFICTION

Dear Memory: Letters on Writing, Silence, and Grief

FOR CHILDREN

Love, Love
Is Mommy?

ANTHOLOGIES

Asian American Poetry: The Next Generation

ERRATUM

Due to a printing error, the lines of the poem on page 10 were broken incorrectly. This is how the poem should look:

Mountain, 1960

Agnes tells us to *hold our minds empty and tranquil*
as they are, and recognize our feelings at the same time.

I want to ask Agnes how to do both at once. When my mind is
empty, the feelings are gone. When the feelings are here, my tranquility

is gone. What happens when the mind separates from the feelings, when
all I have left are feelings, when the feelings are ahead of everything, even the

pain it represents? I can't remember when the outside flesh became our only
flesh. When our minds could no longer be minds, could no longer be held still except

by other people's eyes. I have given my mind away. When I ask for it back, I'm handed
something round and dead, but adorned with flashing lights. What's left is not tranquil.

What's left are feelings that can only fit through a thin straw. Meaning they must be small, in
pieces, and consumable. Maybe the present is so loud because we grow up thinking the future

is possible, but soon realize we are estranged from it, just as we are estranged from the ocean.

WITH MY BACK TO THE WORLD

WITH MY BACK TO THE WORLD

POEMS

VICTORIA CHANG

Farrar, Straus and Giroux

New York

Farrar, Straus and Giroux
120 Broadway, New York 10271

Library of Congress Cataloging-in-Publication Data
Names: Chang, Victoria, 1970– author.
Title: With my back to the world : poems / Victoria Chang.
Description: First edition. | New York : Farrar, Straus and Giroux, 2024.
Identifiers: LCCN 2023041415 | ISBN 9780374611132 (hardcover)
Subjects: LCGFT: Poetry.
Classification: LCC PS3603.H3575 W58 2024 | DDC 811/.6—dc23/eng/20231006
LC record available at https://lccn.loc.gov/2023041415

Designed by Gretchen Achilles

Our books may be purchased in bulk for promotional, educational,
or business use. Please contact your local bookseller or the Macmillan
Corporate and Premium Sales Department at 1-800-221-7945, extension 5442,
or by email at MacmillanSpecialMarkets@macmillan.com.

www.fsgbooks.com
Follow us on social media at @fsgbooks

To my family

I

II

III

With My Back to the World, 1997

This year I turned my back to the world. I let language face

the front. The parting felt like a death. The first person ran away like a horse. When the first person left, there was no

second or third person as I had originally thought. All that remained was repetition. And blue things. This year I stopped shaking the rain off of umbrellas and nothing bad happened.

The terror of this year was emptiness. But I learned that it's

possible for a sentence to have no words. That the meaning of a word can exist without the word. That life can still occur

without a mind. That emptiness still swarms without the world. That it can be disconnected from the wall and still

light up. The best thing about emptiness is if you close your eyes in a field, you'll open your eyes in a field.

On a clear day, the horses disappeared. Just the apples they had been fed were left. The apples were strewn across the field and had became rectangles. When people found them, they still gathered and ate them. The people who hunched over their apples were far away. But the sounds of their chewing were over here. On a clear day, all the sounds fit into the boxes. On any clear day, all my thinking fits into boxes that can't be opened. What if our thinking was never meant to come out? What if our thinking only remains thinking within boxes? When out, they become weapons, take on different shapes with sharp points. Today, there is no shortage of thinking but all the thinking is divided into portions. Today, I am hungry but all the portions are gone, there are only forty eight. On some clear days, there are only forty eight birds and forty eight people and forty eight houses. And forty eight wars. And forty eight apples. I keep counting grids. But no matter how I try, I still get six dead Asian women who fit into forty eight boxes. All night, my thoughts are shaped liked birds. In the morning, I lean in closer to the mirror and someone has drawn lines across my face. I realize failure consists of both the outline and the outlined. I realize the lines have not abandoned us, but just our emptiness inside.

On a Clear Day, 1973

On a clear day, the horses disappeared. Just the apples they had been fed were left. The apples were strewn

across the field and had become rectangles. When people found them, they still gathered and ate them. The

people who hunched over their apples were far away. But the sounds of their chewing were over here. On

a clear day, all the sounds fit into the boxes. On any clear day, all my thinking fits into boxes that can't be opened.

What if our thinking was never meant to come out? If it only remains thinking within boxes?

When out, it becomes weapons, takes on different shapes with sharp points. Today, there is no shortage

of thinking but all the thinking is divided into portions. Today, I am hungry but all the portions are gone, there are

only 48. On clear days there are only 48 birds, 48 people, and 48 houses. And 48 wars.

And 48 apples. I keep counting grids. But no matter how I try, I still get

6 dead Asian women who don't fit into 48 boxes. All night, my thoughts are shaped like birds. In the

morning, I lean in closer to the mirror and someone has drawn lines across my face. I realize that failure consists of

both the outline and the outlined. That lines are not meant to hold in our emptiness.

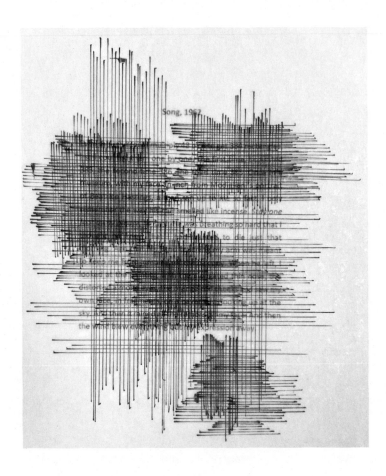

Song, 1962

Even though I could multiply 48 by 8 to get 384 rectangles, I still counted them one by one. The first time, I counted 383, the second time 386, the third time and all the times after, I couldn't count past my age. Once in a museum, with my face an inch from Modigliani's portrait of Beatrice Hastings, a man ran up to me so fast, I only remember the way his hair smelled like incense. *Stay one foot away please*, he said. He was breathing so hard that I thought he knew that I had wanted to die just that morning. And that his hand touching my arm was meant to keep me from jumping off the balcony. When he left, I looked at the painting with the elongated thin nose, the distorted almond eyes, the orange-red cheeks and saw my own face, in fragments, on a pavement, looking up at the sky. And then it rained all the rumors off my face. And then the wind blew everything but my expression away.

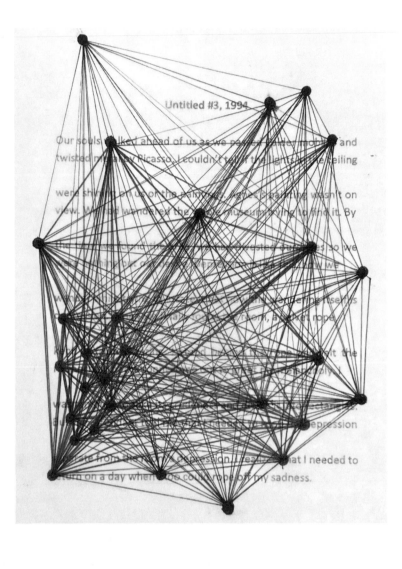

Untitled #3, 1994

Our souls walked ahead of us as we _____ _____ and twisted my way Picasso. I couldn't tell the _____ the ceiling were shining upon the painting, _____ painting wasn't on view. We _____ wandered the _____ trying to find it. By _____

_____ depression separate from _____ depression I realized that I needed to return on a day where _____ could rope off my sadness.

Untitled #3, 1994

Our souls walked ahead of us as we passed Calder mobiles and
twisted metal by Picasso. I couldn't tell if the lights in the ceiling

were shining on us or the paintings. Agnes's painting wasn't on
view. We had wandered the whole museum trying to find it. By

the time we found the area, we had divested ourselves so we
were nothing but our desire. Depression is like this, how we

wander while trying to locate it but how the wandering itself is
depression. When we finally found the room, a velvet rope

kept us from entering. I stood behind the rope and felt the
melancholy of the room come out to greet my melancholy. I

was tempted to take its crudeness and divide it into rectangles.
But the attendant told me that I needed to keep my depression

separate from the room's depression. I realized that I needed to
return on a day when I too could rope off my sadness.

Mountain, 1960

Agnes tells us to *hold our minds empty and tranquil*
as they are, and recognize our feelings at the same time.

I want to ask Agnes how to do both at once.
When my mind is empty, the feelings are gone.
When the feelings are here, my tranquility

is gone. What happens when the mind separates from the
feelings, when all I have left are feelings, when the
feelings are ahead of everything, even the

pain it represents? I can't remember when the outside flesh
became our only flesh. When our minds could no longer
be minds, could no longer be held still except

by other people's eyes. I have given my mind away.
When I ask for it back, I'm handed something round and dead,
but adorned with flashing lights. What's left is not tranquil.

What's left are feelings that can only fit through a thin straw.
Meaning they must be small, in pieces, and consumable.
Maybe the present is so loud because we grow up thinking the future

is possible, but soon realize we are estranged from it,
just as we are estranged from the ocean.

There are 1645 boxes. Inside each box is a small white dot. On some days ████████ like a dot. On other days, each dot is one of ███████████ tears in the last week. Mary Ruefle kept a ██████████ is here, in these squares. I now know ████████████ unborn. In Chinese, ██████ is different from ███████ first means *heart hurts*. The second means ███████████ *uncomfortable*. In English, we say ████████████ language, the heart can be in pa████████████ pain. It is not a small mammal ████████████████████ they do not come not ███████████████████████ ████████████████████████████ or us ██████████████████████████████ an ████████████████████████████████ co███████████████████████████████ ██████████████████████████████

Summer, 1964

There are 1,645 boxes. Inside each box is a small white dot. On some days, the dot looks like a dot. On other days, each dot is one of my tears. 1,645 tears in the last week. Mary Ruefle kept a *cryalog*. My log is here, in these squares. I now know that tears aren't stillborn. In Chinese, 心疼 is different from 心裡難受. The first means *heart hurts*. The second means *heart inside is uncomfortable*. In English, we say *my heart aches*. In every language, the heart can be in pain. But the heart doesn't feel pain. It is not a small mammal. Tears do not come from the heart. They do not come from the eyes, or the body. They come from outside of us like time, from one large repository, which is why we cry when other people cry. In this way, tears are communal. We depend on each other for our sadness.

Friendship, 1963

My desk points in the direction of the ocean but I can't see
it. I have hung up a blue curtain instead of the ocean. But all
I see is a whale. This is the problem of imagination. It has no
shape and comes for no reason. It might not change the imag-
iner or the thing itself, but the person you tell it to. The people
on the other side of the wall sit at a table that faces east. From
above, the crows only see small dots. Agnes said, *In solitude
there is consolation thinking of others and myself, even plants. I
am immediately apprehensive because my solitude has been in-
terrupted.* What am I to do with the people on the other side of
the wall? The friendships that take hold in me like headlights.
Can a person be anything but an intrusion? A train about to
burn in my body. All friendships are cut flowers. Dissertations
on misunderstanding. I see no friends here, just 1,776 depres-
sions. All gold-leafed. Proof that something can be too much
to bear and also glitter. The problem with depression is that
someone else made it, but that person never existed.

Untitled #10, 2002

What happens if these aren't pastoral or war poems? When I can feel the light I carry on my back but can't see it or use it?

When sadness and language cast the same shadow. These six strips are the shadows of our blood, proving that every woman's life can

be broken into and displayed. On some nights, if I zoom in to the painting, they become three sets of lips. If I hold my phone near

my mouth, I can feel three people breathing on my face. I made an effort to unlove everyone but all I received were these lips, slightly

open. Today my 80-year-old neighbor told me, *Everything hurts . . . you'll see.* I wanted to tell him that I already see. After a

death, the idea of a journey disappears. After two deaths, the journey doubles. Maybe our bodies never had a vanishing point,

so there will always be hunger. Even a woman's life is trying to become more than the woman it represents.

Starlight, 1962

Suppose the stars are just our grief reflected back to us, proof that grief sometimes forgets its source, that it can find dead things no matter how distant. Everyone arrives one day and asks, *is this it?* And the stars answer back with more stars. I wonder if Agnes started at the bottom or at the top, if she went left to right or right to left. There's no use in wondering if the canvas was on the floor or on a table. To ask questions is to be distracted by point of view. Point of view has a terrible memory. I've looked at photos scrolling up and over, zooming in and out, and realize it is not love I want, just the ability to zoom back out. A woman loses herself when she can no longer zoom out. Agnes knew that love exists because of the distance of starlight. That desire is the only thing with nerve endings. That it drips. That it dries faster in the desert. She knew to paint it vertically but to hang it horizontally.

I wo

Little Sister

I woke up • at three a.m. because • I felt some of the • brass nails in my brain moving • They have begun to rust but • are still in their original places • There are 364 nails • in my head • The last nail • the 365th is • in my heart to hold it in place • The last nail is bent and • the rust has turned red • On some days • I wake up at • two a.m. and pull • the nail out as the heart sags • like remorse • When I pull it off • I can still feel • proving that the heart never did • what we thought it did • I realized this morning at four a.m. • that I have begun to chase • the words of every person who • will still look at me • Ruefle says *now men look right through me* • *as if I have become a ghost* • *That I no longer exist* • The crows knew this would happen • so they never gave us attention • *Gave us attention* implies • attention needs a philanthropist • I learn today that birds in the sky • don't have shadows • The birds tell me at the • gate that I will need to turn • in my attention • which I now know is the last nail that held • my heart in place • And on the other side • the hearts are no longer held up • lie on the ground • exposed • sunning like old medallions

Buds, 1959

Grieving starts long before we're born. Which is why we're born with 35 buds of sadness. The buds begin to fade at our birth. I only have three buds left because I sold most of my grief already. I have been holding my breath for years and when I finally breathe out, there are people at my door waiting to collect my breathing in jars to sell. When I tell them I don't want to sell what's left, they bring jars of moonlight for my poems for $12 each. I buy one because the people look like Girl Scouts and are pulling a wagon. When they turn, I can see that they have tails. When I put the moon in a poem, it quivers like a strobe light nearly out of batteries. Once a dying woman said *goodbye* on Twitter right before she died. Sometimes I go onto the accounts of dead people and read their final posts. I listen to music while scrolling. The people singing in my ears are also dead. It is getting harder to be born and to vanish at once. Isn't this what we all wanted anyway?

On a Clear Day

Agnes said her   from the   *trees.* I've   thought trees
grids came   *innocence of*   always   were guilty.

They never   can never say   somewhere   they didn't
have an alibi,   they were   else or that   witness the

murders. Is this   to cut out   and dismantle   morning, I
why I desire   Agnes's grids   them? Each   enter the yard

and wait for   speak back to   50th year   finally realize
the trees to   me. This is my   doing so. I   that the trees

won't tell   there is no   a life. It is only   a final draft,
me. That   first draft of   and always   the rectangles

drawn as we   the same as   though some   tried to be like
go. Each one   the others,   years may have   a circle. This is

by design, so   looks back at a   remember are   divided
that when one   life, all we   the equal and   sadnesses.

Aspiration, 1960

Aspiration looks the same, from row to row, slightly slanted to the right. As a child, we started at the bottom left. Now I am somewhere in the third section out of four. Looking up, nothing changes. With aspiration,

everything above is the same as everything below. I still hope for a stranger future, one without a hole. A woman's canal is a gate to more gates that look the same. And at the end, the gate is a parallelogram

because life leans to the right from all the repetition. So we continue to aspire, from one space into the next, barefoot, but always trying to leave a trace. No one will ever get asked one question: *why not stay?* Most of us

are stuck here in these grids, counting memory. In this room, I am trying to paint in lowercase. I am trying to draw a woman's heartbeat, not the heart. The sensation of being strangled, not the hands around my neck.

Grass, 1967

When I open the door, I smile and wave to people who only have eyes and who are infinitely joyful. I see my children, but only the backs of their heads. When they turn around, I don't recognize them. They once had mouths but now only have eyes. I want to leave the room but when I do, I am outside, and everyone else is inside. So next time, I open the door and stay inside. But then everyone is outside. Agnes said that *solitude and freedom are the same*. My solitude is like the grass. I become so aware of its presence that it too begins to feel like an audience. Sometimes my solitude grabs my phone and takes a selfie, posts it somewhere for others to see and like. Sometimes people comment on how beautiful my solitude is and sometimes my solitude replies with a heart. It begins to follow the accounts of solitudes that are half its age. What if my solitude is depressed? What if even my solitude doesn't want to be alone?

Untitled, 1961

Agnes's lines desire to touch each other, but never can. Depression is a group of parallel lines that want to touch, but never can. Or maybe it is a group of parallel lines that only other people hope will touch. If I look closely with a magnifying glass, a few lines almost meet. Maybe the magnifying glass gets tired of seeing everything for what it is. Agnes left a small triangle empty at the top. Is the triangle empty or is it the shape that's actually filled in? Is the rest of the triangle, with its hundreds of lines, actually empty? Maybe the earth is empty and the sky is full. Maybe life is only a holding room before death. Maybe we were deposited here because we were the ones tagged as having an ego. The others are somewhere else in space, without consciousness.

Falling Blue, 1963

Someone wrote that Agnes made small simple repetitive gestures that led to something larger. This resembles a life, each day a mark on canvas. Or the way a prisoner might carve each day on a wall. On some days, I think about putting down the brush. On other days, I want so badly to finish so I can see the complete piece. No one tells you that you'll never see your own painting because you'll be dead. What we make can only be seen by someone else. What can I learn from these other paintings? Besides that a man can never see us because he is an inch from his own canvas. Besides that each line does eventually end but will always be unfinished. It's three a.m. and a small light shines on my paper. A dog snores on my dead mother's green chair. At this hour, a line is the thing with a human face. There is no hope in shapes. There is just the line and the sound of its scratch as it crosses out memory. Perhaps it's not memory we're trying to capture, but everything instead of it.

White Stone, 1965

I can almost see Agnes's tiny lines on the canvas. The lines are not agreeable. They measure nothing. Agnes said to *make happiness your goal*. I can see the lines best if I am one foot away. The desire to die is 13 inches away. Agnes said that an artist must *think the work is paramount in your life*. I want to ask Agnes how to do this but I cannot move. I want to ask her how to move away from her painting and not die. How to back away and not seek the attention of the first person I see. The stranger staring at another painting looks like a nice person. If I step away, will Agnes's lines hold me back like a net? Keep me from conjugating every person I meet? From trying to capitalize numbers? As I step back though, everything changes. I no longer see the lines but just a tone. This must be what dying feels like. Or knowledge.

The Islands, 1961

At first, I just notice the small white dots in pairs that look like holes. But then I see the pencil grid underneath. Suddenly, I remember that there is a middle of the day. I've spent years considering the beginning or ending. The dots hold on, small headlights looking out at me. Why keep the grids after they have been used? This has something to do with desire. How to reconcile the fact that I want to make art but don't want to be criticized. That I want to be loved but I don't want to open my mouth. That I want to be saved but I don't want to kneel down. Pessoa said, *In order to understand, I destroyed myself.* The dots are on the lines, not in the rectangles, as if to say that beauty must destroy something. Agnes left some lines uncovered on the borders, showing us how happiness is made. How even happiness is made by writing something down, then leaving it exposed for all to see. Is it possible to be seen, but not looked at?

Drift of Summer, 1964

Agnes drew 44 lines vertically, 33 lines horizontally. Sometimes the ink thickens at the end of the line into a dot. I imagine her hand anticipating the ending, looking at the point and beyond at the same time. I'm afraid to follow the lines to their ends because there might be nothing after or maybe something after is more terrifying. Is it possible to feel happiness while on the line? Or is the present just the pointed tip of death's sword? Even though the handoff is seamless, I still want to see it happen. There was a time when we didn't think about happiness, when it was possible not to think about something because there was no word for it yet. Then perhaps language is ruin. Agnes said, *in all the arts, technique is a hazard even as it is in living life*. Then what are we to do with language? Once the whales are gone, an ocean isn't an ocean anymore. And then we get to rename it.

I counted 44 lines and while I counted, 44 Asian women were assaulted. Agnes said she was not a woman. If Agnes was not a woman, how did she know this is the color of desire? To be a woman is to be seen as a woman. To be able to hear a child growing but being unable to help myself grow. To be able to have ideas but being unable to lift my ideas over the wall on my own. It's August finally and no one knows that August isn't really a month. It is one long day. We assume Asian women are made of flowers, but some of us are made up of lines. It's hard to say when these lines were no longer just themselves. The minute Agnes put the brush to the canvas, they became indescribable. The sayable, by nature, is an elegy. The unsayable, outside of time. The challenge of writing is that I am trying to say the unsayable while inside of someone else's idea of time.

Untitled IX, 1982

I counted 44 lines and while I counted, 44 Asian women were touched. People confused the 44 Asian women with each other. How did Agnes know this is the color of desire? To be an Asian woman is to be seen as night. To be able to hear a child growing but being unable to help myself. To be able to have ideas but being unable to lift them over the wall on my own. It's August finally and no one knows that August isn't really a month. It is one long day. Some people assume Asian women are made of flowers, but some of us are made up of lines. It's hard to say when these lines were no longer just themselves. The minute Agnes put the brush to the canvas, they became indescribable. The sayable, by nature, is an elegy. The unsayable, outside of time. What we say, here, now, is only the part of flesh that is known.

The Tree, 1964

Today I walked with two poets through a small forest. The bugs kept yelling questions. When I tried to answer, they denied asking me the questions. The air is so wet here that it only knows how to touch my lips assertively. The bugs are loudest behind me. They sound like fractions of pain, like Agnes's tree which is visible because of its parts. But what do the darker lines mean? Before I arrived to this city, I could feel the depression in my fingertips. It made my fingers tingle. Sadness is the most alive emotion. It gets into your nerves. Its pulses feel like insects at the rim of your skin. If I turn the canvas on its side, the lines look like my depression stacking. I quickly turn it back to the way Agnes intended. Now that I've seen the tree on its side, I am no longer afraid of vanishing. The insects are now in front of me but they face me. I used to think depression was all around me, that I was within it. Now I see that it is always ahead of me. That it is in pieces, but it moves in a swarm.

Untitled, 1960

Agnes drew 15 semicircles on each double line. The trouble with 15 is that it can only make 7 circles. What happens to the final semicircle? It is always

there. Depression is the final semicircle. It is the first, second, and third person. It grabs all the perspectives. The only other

thing like this is a wave. All of that pushing and the water never made it anywhere. The semicircles look like writing on lined paper. I am writing

these words on lined paper to see if it's possible to write my way out of the moon. Agnes threw away any art she made that she didn't like. I just

went to the ocean with a basket of poems and tried to give them away. Even the ocean didn't want them, blew them back into my face. The

letters hit me so hard, they changed the shape of my nose. But I still felt the urge to show someone something. Maybe these aren't semicircles.

Maybe they are one long string, made into small even humps. If I pull one end, my depression will flatten, but my words will also disappear.

Fiesta, 1985

Agnes said that painting is not about *ideas or personal emotion*, that the object is *freedom*. The 6 thicker lines seem to dominate, but it's the 12 thin lines between them that I can't stop looking at, because of their silence, their near disappearance. Yesterday, when I looked out the front window, I thought I saw a thick rope at the end of the driveway. When I looked again later, it was gone. Once something is written, it disappears. Before anything is written, it is completely possible. Once the line is drawn, the light narrows to a pinhole. What is art but trying to make something resemble what it was before it was made, when it was still unknown and free? The desire to draw a line is to ask a rhetorical question. All future lines are an attempt to answer that question. This year, I scribbled things down that I could read, that made sense to me, but no one else could understand. I wrote for an entire year and when I looked up, the ocean was dry, some men were signing more treaties, and the moon had been sold at auction.

Untitled #12, 1981

Agnes must have wanted me to see innocence or happiness
when looking at this painting. But all I see is the gathering

of pink at the bottom. For every woman, there is a man who
is nearby. Every woman has asked a tree a question. If you

ask a tree too many questions, it will fall down. You can hear

a tree take its last breath, it sounds like gurgling. All the
answers are in the gurgling. A woman just shut a window

because of someone staring in. I can't look at the window

without thinking *man*. Or *kidnap*. Or *knife*. I prefer the words
of things I can't see, such as *wind, now, exist*. Is it possible to

separate a woman from her life? For a life to just be a life?
For the art to be down the road from the paint? Just once I
want to look in the mirror and wonder, *What is that?*

Leaves, 1966

On some days, my depression is over there in a picnic basket while I am over here looking at art. On those days, I can't control it but at least it's covered, on a lawn, away for a while. On those days, the ants are closer

to my depression than I am. When one finds it, it sends all the ants to it. They cut up my depression, lift it away to feed a queen. Somehow, the queen doesn't get depressed after eating it. But after they're done, I still feel it the next day. Agnes must have miscalculated. There are 127 lines

but only 3 complete sets of 4. The set on the top of the painting only has 3 lines. I miscalculated my depression. The last time I saw it was at 10:00 p.m. I always think it's gone. But it regrows each night. It has skin. It is even waterproof. In that way, it resembles leaves. But everything resembles

leaves at some point, the way they need a host, the way they are called *leaf*, whether they are on a tree or not, their arrival and decay. Maybe that's what we're all doing. Language isn't actually inside us as I had thought. We are tenants of language. We are leaving while writing.

Gratitude, 2001

The red strip is not a tongue or fire. I try to imagine it without

the white strip above it. Or the green blocks. What is the red
strip without anything else? Agnes said *suffering is necessary
for freedom from suffering*. Maybe the yellow strips are
suffering. See how far away they are? Always distant but
always there. Or maybe they are language, in how we can

still see the yellow on the periphery when we look at the red
in the middle. I want to pull the yellow closer but maybe I

should push it away. What am I outside of language? Is this
the solitude Agnes spoke of—standing in an auditorium
without a microphone or an audience, at a podium read-
ing wind. And where the skin that has been wound tightly
around me my whole life, is also the thing that I've been

writing on. To think, everyone will write one final word.

II

Today

—On Kawara's *Today* Series

Jan.4.2022
A call is just a call. I pick it up.

Jan.5.2022
I thought I had a heart inside my heart.

Jan.6.2022
I lift blankets looking for my father.

Jan.7.2022
When I take off the patch, your eye is gone.
I spend the day in other people's tears.

Jan.8.2022

Jan.9.2022
Someone says your eyelid almost came off,
the doctors tried to reattach it. I
close my eye all day to see if I can
feel your dying. What is dying but a
form of hunger, visible to God. When
we pull down your shirt, your good eye opens.
All the waiting, the moon is an athlete.

Jan.10.2022
I rub your stomach like a child. I know
you can't feel it. Later, I rub my own
stomach and feel my dying, it is soft.

Jan.11.2022
The woman who let you fall won't look at
me. In each of us, there is a stranger,
a single road that in one instant forks.

Jan.12.2022
There's a name for it. The way your mouth stays

Today

—On Kawara's *Today* Series

Jan.4.2022
A call is just a call. I pick it up.

Jan.5.2022
I thought I had a heart inside my heart.

Jan.6.2022
I lift blankets looking for my father.

Jan.7.2022
When I take off the patch, your eye is gone.
I spend the day in other people's tears.

Jan.8.2022
They say today could be the day. The geese
will be back later this year, but you will
miss them loosening from the sky. To leave
the earth is to go down a slope one last
time, not look back, each memory stranded.

Jan.9.2022
Someone says your eyelid almost came off,
the doctors tried to reattach it. I
close my eye all day to see if I can
feel your dying. What is dying but a
form of hunger, visible to God. When
we pull down your shirt, your good eye opens.
All the waiting, the moon is an athlete.

Jan.10.2022
I rub your stomach like a child. I know

you can't feel it. Later, I rub my own
stomach and feel my dying, it is soft.

Jan.11.2022
The woman who let you fall won't look at
me. In each of us, there is a stranger,
a single road that in one instant forks.

Jan.12.2022
There's a name for it. The way your mouth stays
open, no breathing. We hold our breaths as
if companions of your dying. *Cheyne-Stokes*,
named after two doctors. What if we named
everything? The last hand squeeze before death,
the way your eye looks at me when I talk,
the way the reincarnated cry the
most, bewildered by the star's second blink.

Jan.13.2022
I tell a story about something, with
my arms waving. And your arm grabs mine, as
if I am a messiah. But really
I withheld food and drink from you so that
your feet that loved to walk would never touch
the ground again. And I wonder why we
are always on our hind legs, to see what?

Jan.14.2022
I read, *For beauty is nothing but the
beginning of terror.* And you make a
face. Your teeth covered in God's vines, dirty,
black. As if to disagree with Rilke.
The rats in the attic have gone. As if
to say terror is the beginning of

beauty. Yesterday, when you opened your
eyes, I moved my face over yours to catch
your viewing of the angels. Your eye popped
open so large that I saw your pupil
and what was behind it this whole time. An
angel, but not a white one. No, this one
was a color I'd never seen before.

Jan.15.2022
Maybe we feel dizzy because we are
moving and so is the earth. On some days,
I can tell the earth is rotating in
another direction. Today I meet
a hospice nurse named Harsh. He is sweet, sweet.

Jan.16.2022
They drop the morphine under your tongue. How
it must feel like a faint raindrop taken
from the sky. It's been two weeks since the fall
and death still catches me by surprise.
I feel nothing. It is raining morphine.

Jan.17.2022
No matter how I scold you, you won't die.
Meanwhile, there are no birds in the sky, they
have all flown into your brain. I always
knew that our thoughts were birds, but I didn't
know they would return for the funeral.

Jan.18.2022
Five breaths. Then a minute of not breathing.
I time it, announce it, as if you are
running a race. You would have loved winning
this race to annihilation. Because

you are winning, your mouth is shaped like an O,
has been open for fourteen days now, as
if to say you aren't done telling me
that Rilke's *Open* doesn't exist, that
our eyes aren't inverted, that we can see
everything an animal sees with our
eyes closed and our mouths open. If I lean in,
I can hear all the words said in your
life, now in a different order. There's still
no *love*, even though I've looked through all the
words twice. I go digging in the mass grave
of language for the extra *love*s and I
end up bringing *loneliness* back with me.

Jan.19.2022
Every phone call says the same thing, that *he
is hanging on*. And I imagine you
holding on to the edge of a building,
the city's mouths waiting for you to jump.

Jan.20.2022
Today is your birthday. Someone came in
and said, *they're still not feeding him?*, thinking
I was someone else. The eyes press against
the glass of my brain. They can't touch me but
they won't stop looking. Eyeballs have footsteps
too. When they walk, they sound sticky. Hundreds
of them have gathered outside the window.

Jan.21.2022

At night, when you stop breathing, you open
your eye that looks like stained glass in the dark.

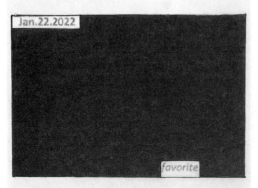

Jan.22.2022

favorite

Jan.23.2022
They called me at 4:30 am and
I don't remember what they said. But I
know they never said the word *death* or *died*.

Jan.24.2022
The funeral home calls and I open
your checkbook, a balance of mocking birds.

Jan.25.2022
What do I do with the photos of my
father's swollen hands? His bloody eye that
never opened again. And the stitchwork
of the surgeon. To love something is to
want to own it. Once I loved my father,
but I always wanted my feelings back.

Jan.26.2022
On my notebook, a large group of ants. I
wonder why they had only gathered there
and on Etel Adnan's, *Time*. They walk on
these words: *When no one is waiting for us
any longer, there's death, so faithful.* I
spend the morning killing ants and wonder
how many insects I have killed until
now. All the killing to prepare me to
forgo the feeding tube. Yesterday I
drove past a group of boys running without
their shirts. At the stoplight I could only

At night, when you stop breathing, you open
your eye that looks like stained glass in the dark.

Jan.22.2022
The sky is crooked at my feet. I'm tired
of someone else's dying. I've lost two
pounds because I've been chewing rain instead
of swallowing it. Because you haven't
been eating or drinking, all the food I
eat tastes twice as dead. Twice as good. In the
room down the hall, a man has a stroke, half
of his body splits off. The caretakers
gossip. My sister won't stop crying, keeps
telling everyone she was your *favorite*.

Jan.23.2022
They called me at 4:30 a.m. and
I don't remember what they said. But I
know they never said the word *death* or *died*.

Jan.24.2022
The funeral home calls and I open
your checkbook, a balance of mocking birds.

Jan.25.2022
What do I do with the photos of my
father's swollen hands? His bloody eye that
never opened again. And the stitchwork
of the surgeon. To love something is to
want to own it. Once I loved my father,
but I always wanted my feelings back.

Jan.26.2022
On my notebook, a large group of ants. I

wonder why they had only gathered there
and on Etel Adnan's *Time*. They walk on
these words: *When no one is waiting for us
any longer, there's death, so faithful*. I
spend the morning killing ants and wonder
how many insects I have killed until
now. All the killing to prepare me to
forgo the feeding tube. Yesterday I
drove past a group of boys running without
their shirts. At the stoplight I could only
see the way their sweat lifted from them. And
I realized the ants weren't coming from the
floor but were coming from my words. Down the
road, another group of runners going
in the opposite direction, having
no idea of the other runners. All
this time, I thought I didn't know a thing.

Jan.27.2022
When death was near, I could touch time. It was
softer than I thought it would be. There were
two of them. When I tried to measure their
lengths, I was sent back to the living. I
was shorter but my shadow was longer.

Jan.28.2022
I walk into someone else's grief. It's
not that different from riding on a
bullet train. It's impossible to see
the decapitated tulip on a
porch. Or the way a bird feeder, empty
and spinning, becomes a thin line. Maybe
the death itself is the epiphany.

Jan.29.2022
The ants are back. When I see them, I want
to kill them right away, and when I do,
I am wide awake from killing. Nothing
can take me from my focus. A murder
of crows flies over me. Once I followed
them to a tree and watched them grieving a
dead crow. Thirty of them yelling into
the sky. I let my father die alone.

Jan.30.2022
One obituary struck me—a young
handsome man, in his thirties. He died with
his brother at his side, it said, and I
wondered about the logistics. Where were
the other people? Were they taking turns?
Was his brother actually *at his side*? How
much more real this sounds: *Mitchell died on June
3, 2022, all alone, in
a hospital bed with heaven pointing
down, having reversed itself in the night.
Everyone else was tired so they went
home to sleep in their own beds because they
knew they would wake up, would have to wake up,
appear when prompted by the sky, to live.*

Jan.31.2022
I read you ten poems, eight-hundred-fifty-
nine lines, I had fourteen coffees, nine cremes,
twenty-three bobas. I cried zero times.

Feb.1.2022
Another day went by. Still no feeling.
Why is language the only thing I have?

I wonder if it's possible to live
by persistence, wanting so badly to
remain secured to the body, that his
soul left fourteen years before its vessel.
When asked when a painting was done, Rothko
said, *there's tragedy in every brushstroke.*

Feb.2.2022
I haven't seen an ant for days. But I
know they're somewhere underground, just as death
is somewhere beyond the door. Or how my
feelings remain elsewhere. I think about
hierarchies—to withhold water from a
father but not from a daughter. When we
stopped giving my father water, I felt
thirsty all day. *I would never* means you've
never had to do it. Two ants appeared
on the ledge, but I couldn't find a source.
Maybe these ants are sadness. And they can't
be killed because they eat their own feelings.

Feb.3.2022
A man from the funeral home called me.
His voice was so flat, I took a nap while
he talked. When I woke up, I was in the
casket looking up at the ceiling fan.
I couldn't move my body and a patch
covered my left eye. I heard my own voice
describing my fall onto a knob, how
I lost my left eye, how I refused to

die. And then I saw myself bend over
to look at me. My own hand grabbed my hand
but I couldn't feel it or move my eye.
I saw myself for who I was—evil,
full of syllables. Poets are useless.

Feb.4.2022
Twice now I've thought about the wood casket
and what proportion of the ashes are
wood. Twice now I've read about the chamber,
this time I learn it is called a *retort*,
also a sharp reply. This time, I read
about the *pugilistic stance* when they
burn the body, the boxer-like pose the
body makes. I think about my father,
alone in the retort, in a small box,
two thousand degrees, his legs bent, his fists
ready to punch me and my live flesh.

Feb.5.2022
Someone said my poems are *incredibly
clear*. Out the window, in the field, seven
cows now gather. When I looked ten minutes
ago, only three cows. What does it mean
to count cows and to name them? Everyone
must know that to be clear means to have lost
something we have loved. Adolf Loos said that
ornament is a crime. No wonder why
the black cows here keep moving in and out
of the window frame. They know someone
has died and landscape is reversible.

Feb.6.2022

die. And then I saw myself bend over
to look at me. My own hand grabbed my hand
but I couldn't feel it or move my eye.
I saw myself for who I was—evil,
full of syllables. Poets are useless.

Feb.4.2022
Twice now I've thought about the wood casket
and what proportion of the ashes are
wood. Twice now I've read about the chamber,
this time I learn it is called a *retort*,
also a sharp reply. This time, I read
about the *pugilistic stance* when they
burn the body, the boxer-like pose the
body makes. I think about my father,
alone in the retort, in a small box,
two thousand degrees, his legs bent, his fists
ready to punch me and my live flesh.

Feb.5.2022
Someone said my poems are *incredibly
clear*. Out the window, in the field, seven
cows now gather. When I looked ten minutes
ago, only three cows. What does it mean
to count cows and to name them? Everyone
must know that to be clear means to have lost
something we have loved. Adolf Loos said that
ornament is a crime. No wonder why
the black cows here keep moving in and out
of the window frame. They know someone
has died and landscape is reversible.

Feb.6.2022
The cows have spread out and I have counted

fourteen. Their heads always hang down. They don't
seem to need to look up. In that way, they
are unlike us. Our euphoria that
comes directly from despair. *Look up*, we
say, to remind us that we will all die.
Here, the sky is made of nothing. It is
so vast that the twenty-five people who
live here don't have enough sight to change it.

Feb.7.2022
I have experienced death twice now, and
maybe this is the last time since we can't
know our own. The sky isn't a threshold
because it reveals everything, there is
nowhere to hide. All the syntax is there.
The birds here must have longer wings, to push
down the epiphanies from other states.
Today, a hawk, a goose, and an eagle
flew above me at once. Their wings pushed down
so much blue that my boots sunk down an inch.
Now that no one is left, there is nothing
left to know. There was never joy in life,
only varying lengths of sadness, in
between the cows, birds, and our looking up.

Feb.8.2022
It turns out the hawk is an eagle, a
young one, and the sound of its wings isn't
advice or something errant. They are just
wings today, without subject matter or
an afterlife. Just this, today, now. Once
the bird moves out of the window frame, it
no longer exists. Finally, a white
truck passes through the first frame, then the next.

The sun rescinds its light on the hillside
so I no longer fear the pink tips, so
that I am so calm I fall asleep in
the armchair, just like my father on day
four of his dying. I know my mouth is
wide open, like his, all the words that came
out and then didn't. Somehow I think all
the words of the dead are here, except *death*.

Feb.9.2022
Today they burned my father. A man named
Garrett called me, in his toneless voice, to
say that someone cleaned his body, covered
him in white linen. After the man called,
I felt warmer all day. My body reached
two thousand degrees but would not burn. I
realized I had not thought of my father
more than once in Wyoming. You'd never
know the planet is dying. Here, the clouds
have holes in them and the deer are more etched
with shadow. A sandwich arrives at my
door at noon. I'm so hungry that I eat
the sandwich first, then think of my father.

Feb.10.2022
Today the river is in crisis, no
horizon dares to go near it. Today
my father is in a small jar. At dusk,
I went into a painter's studio,
saw his stretched canvas on the table, white,
empty. What are we without those who made
us? *May his memory be your blessing*,
people emailed me all week. The artist
was painting a series of doors, which were

so real that I walked through the one that was
slightly open. Inside the room was my
breath that I had held since January
13, an eyelid, a loose eyeball, the
knob the eye fell on, the girl's hands that tried
to catch him, which were charred and still waving.

Feb.11.2022
The white truck went from one frame to the next
and I thought of the time when someone lied
about me. How day and night I cared so
much about the lie that it split into
two, one part went out the left window frame,
the other out the right. Like the blue car
that disappears at the same time as the
white one, yet I can see both at once. When
they burned my father's body, I wondered
if the eyeballs spread so far on each side
that they could see Wyoming, these two panes,
me on a small brown chair, looking out the
windows, waiting for oblivion to
travel through with its eighteen wheels and truth.

Feb.12.2022
At the beginning of our family tree
was hope. Or maybe it was just an owl.

Feb.13.2022
The same wind was blowing here eighty years
ago, always snapping families in half.

Feb.14.2022

If I keep the window closed, I am stuck
inside with language as it buzzes back
and forth, trying to get out and start wars.
My sister is the only one left. If
she is the favorite of nothing, then
I must be one of Calvino's cities,
the one with angular shadows, the one
that when turned on its side, you can see through

Feb.15.2022

The caskets are shaking. The white-tailed deer
gently cross the river. I hike up the
hill to find my feelings. Instead, I run
into Hope, who doesn't look at me or
stop, but walks down the hill. Today could be
a day where everything is beautiful.

Feb.16.2022

Yesterday, I walked to the small chapel,
head down, yet all the people driving by
waved to me as if they knew what I had
just done, as if they knew I was going
to the chapel. When I got there, fourteen
white-tailed deer stopped and stared, moving away
from me, as if they also knew. Inside, the
cold mixed with the cold from my body and
the moment of mixing, the stained glass, and
my sobbing finally came. It was so
delayed that I wasn't sure if I was
crying for the deer that wouldn't stay, or
the nine people I had just met and would
soon leave behind, the snow that would
come after I am gone, or my father.
I left a note in the guest book, wrote his
name. Above it, *Thomas and Claire Bushnell*,
married the day before my father's death,
a tribute to *Traveler, one of the*
best horses ever. It's time to go home.

Feb.17.2022

blossoms

Feb.14.2022
If I keep the window closed, I am stuck
inside with language as it buzzes back
and forth, trying to get out and start wars.
My sister is the only one left. If
she is the favorite of nothing, then
I must be one of Calvino's cities,
the one with angular shadows, the one
that when turned on its side, becomes a line.

Feb.15.2022
The caskets are shaking. The white-tailed deer
gently cross the river. I hike up the
hill to find my feelings. Instead, I run
into Hope, who doesn't look at me or
stop, but walks down the hill. Today could be
a day where everything is beautiful.

Feb.16.2022
Yesterday, I walked to the small chapel,
head down, yet all the people driving by
waved to me as if they knew what I had
just done, as if they knew I was going
to the chapel. When I got there, fourteen
white-tailed deer stopped and stared, moving away
from me, as if they also knew. Inside, the
cold mixed with the cold from my body and
the moment of mixing, the stained glass, and
my sobbing finally came. It was so
delayed that I wasn't sure if I was
crying for the deer that wouldn't stay, or
the nine people I had just met and would
soon leave behind, the snow that would

come after I am gone, or my father.
I left a note in the guest book, wrote his
name. Above it, *Thomas and Claire Bushnell,*
married the day before my father's death,
a tribute to *Traveler, one of the*
best horses ever. It's time to go home.

Feb.17.2022
Each of us comes from somewhere with blossoms.

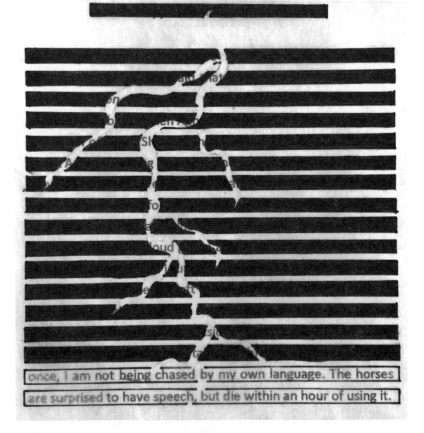

once, I am not being chased by my own language. The horses are surprised to have speech, but die within an hour of using it.

Perfect Happiness
(from Innocent Love Series, 1999)

Agnes believed in living *above the line*. Above the line is *happiness* and *love*. She said that *below the line is all sadness and destruction*. Last year, I moved below the line, into the yellow or the blue. When Agnes left New York, she was fifty-five. She feared *sin of pride*. She tried not to talk for three years. I want to ask Agnes if leaving New York and giving away all her brushes moved her back above the line. I want to ask her what to do if I can't live in solitude for three years. What to do if my daughter cuts herself and her arms look like Agnes's lines. Yesterday on a plane, we passed a cloud group as large as a city. Inside, every few seconds, lightning. I turned my neck as far as possible until I could no longer see it. I left my sight over there. I still see the lightning, even days later. On some nights, I am so below the line that I leave my breathing outside by accident. By the time I realize it, all the horses have taken my breathing and run off. For once, I am not being chased by my own language. The horses are surprised to have speech, but die within an hour of using it.

Innocent Love
(from Innocent Love Series, 1999)

Agnes said that your *conditioning has taught you to identify with others, their emotions and their needs. It is particularly*

difficult for women, but still it has to be done. The purpose of life is to know your true, unconditioned self. I wonder if Agnes meant that innocent love is the kind of love that is within us. I have wanted the kind outside this window. I hear laughter, coins, and music, but when I open the window, I am

somewhere inside intelligence with no signs of life. I used to close the window and the sounds would keep me alive. The only way to see Agnes's unconditioned self is to open the window and hear silence, the thick shafts of blue. This silence must come from before our birth when things didn't have words. There

must be a reason why we look at the mirror and see ourselves, not someone else. Why we see a face, not words.

I Love the Whole World, 2000

When I look at the 16 blue strips, I too love the whole world. But it is 13 days before September 11. There are three extra blue strips that I never know what to do with. Maybe the three blue strips are meaning. Agnes painted this a year before September 11 and *Gratitude* in 2001. In 2001, there was a field, two buildings, three planes. When I held my fingers up to the sun, I used to be able to see

the veins. Now I can't see them because the dead bodies are still in front of the sun. The dead are always gathering around something the wrong scale. Agnes said it is the *scale of the composition* that matters. *If the painting has perfect scale, it moves you.* The sky is always the wrong scale. It's not actually too large, but it's too small. The people on the plane are now the wrong scale. Language is also the wrong scale.

Red Bird, 1964

I've only seen a dead bird up close once. It wasn't red but blue. I named it *Happiness* before I buried it. My child found a few sticks so we could make a cross. We dug a hole and dropped the bird in, along with a few flowers we plucked. We didn't touch the bird with our bare hands, in case death was contagious. When I put the cross into the ground, I felt that Nietzsche was wrong. Happiness isn't the feeling that power increases. The lake isn't a marketplace. The small pencil marks on the painting aren't measuring anything. Seeing the dead bird up close only made me want to cover it, not sell its feelings. I am far away from it, in another house, but I still have the bird's feelings in a small box. Each spring, I can't see the baby birds in the rafters that, when hungry, sound like death. All these months, I thought they were birds, but it turns out they were really rats. And the feelings in the small box were my own.

Untitled, 1960

Agnes incised her grids onto the wet blue wound. Each rectangle is marked twice, with two carats, as if to say the grids aren't enough, that beauty must be scored twice. I used to think that love and death could be separate. That one didn't drag the other. Now I think death is the form of love. My real secret isn't that I have two hearts but that I have two eye colors. My blue eye can see death and my brown eye can see love. The trouble is that looking involves both eyes. When people die, the eyes still want to remain open, to continue stockpiling images. Funeral homes use spiky eye cups to keep the eyes shut. As if a lifetime of sight can be contained. The images after a person dies travel, looking for a new home. Sometimes that home is a painting or an abandoned building. Other times, the images are homeless for so long, they bind together with images from other people and turn into memory.

Untitled, 1978

Agnes once said, *the silence on the floor of my house is all the questions and all the answers that have ever been in the world.* I sit and wait for the floor to speak to me. But it just acts like a floor. The floor never testifies on my behalf even though it has felt everything. Agnes says to give up facts, to *have an empty mind.* That if *your mind is full of garbage, if an inspiration came, you wouldn't recognize it.* Agnes tried to avoid having ideas because they are *inaccurate.* Someone said that *what torments us isn't death, but life.* All along I have been preoccupied with the wrong thing. Maybe the five red bands are life. They wrap around my neck like someone's arms. When Agnes said *you just can't be an artist if you can't be alone,* I dreamt of the Tahoe fire. I, in the middle of it, sparks falling from the sky like men, the ski lift swaying from thoughts. And I woke up, my mind filled with smoke, no people, and Agnes's words. And the floor emptying my thinking like long division.

Untitled #5, 1998

When Agnes came on screen, I thought of all the canvases that still hold her gaze. Maybe a painting is an accumulation

of our gazes and why they sometimes seem human. When I look at the pastel bands, the painting collects my seeing and

sends back a dead person's feelings. I am surprised when the feelings don't feel outdated. Agnes said an artist *needs to be*

alone. What if I've spent my whole life wanting to be seen? In that way, I've wanted to be the painting, not the painter.

But I am the painter. Even now, I walk outside at night just so the sky can see me one more time. Stéphane Mallarmé once

wrote: *Paint not the thing, but the effect it produces*. I have wanted the sky all along, but my wanting was misplaced. I lift

my hand into the air and feel something grabbing my wrist. But it's not the sky, it's the beauty of the sky.

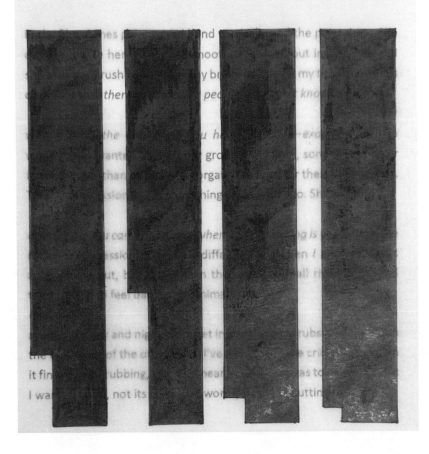

Untitled #10, 1990

Untitled #10, 1990

In the film, Agnes paints a red band vertically and the paint drips. She catches it with her brush and smooths the drips out into the band. I shiver as her brush passes over my brain, flattening my thinking. Agnes once said that *there are so many people who don't know what they*

want. . . . that's the only thing you have to know—exactly what you want. Agnes wanted 11 lines per group or 44 lines, some lines darker in some areas than others. She forgave the lines for their thinning out. Their transgressions have something to do with ego. She said *the*

worst thing you can think about when you're working is yourself. In the midst of depression, there is even a difference between *I* and *me*. Tears never come out, but drip within the body. A small river forms and things begin to feel damp. The animals gather

around. All day and night, a cricket inside my body rubs one wing with the underside of the other wing. I've never seen the cricket, but when it finally stops rubbing, I can still hear it. My error was to become what I wanted to be, not its tone. The words, not their cutting.

Happy Holiday, 1999

Each red band is a different shade of red, with its own ego.
Agnes said *everyone is born a hundred percent ego and*

after that it's all adjustment. These bands are not columns to
hold up cornices. They are not fluted. Turn a column on its side

and all the ideas disappear. Trauma is vertical, not horizontal.
The horizontal line is gentle. The vertical is aggressive.

Surveillance is vertical. War is vertical. A holiday is horizontal.
Unless it's a war holiday, then it's a square. Agnes said *a square*

is overconfident and aggressive. A rectangle is *more relaxed,
softer, and agreeable.* The pain I feel inside my chest is a heart's

change from a square to a rectangle. The stretching hurts. The
pain has something to do with solitude. Today, I finally hear the

rectangle's first words which aren't words exactly. They sound
like something splashing.

Untitled, 2004

I counted 24 days since I first started writing. Love can't be counted or re-created but if I stay out in front of it, I can make space for myself. But then I'm alone, no longer among the living. You urged me to look to myself, not to identify with others,

their emotions, or needs. And I did that for 24 days. Each day, a bird hit my window and reminded me that I once let them in too. If I give too much away, it's not the heart that is depleted but the eyes with all the noticing. My eyes used to take up my entire head. Now they are two dots. It will take a year for them to grow back. But when they do, they will no longer be able to move. You once said, *we are born as nouns not verbs*. I emptied myself for 24 days and I have nothing to show you but two holes.

Hole is still a noun and a verb. So is *desire, stroke, silence*. After 24 days, I am still trying to be a noun. Not *help, question,* or *hope*. Maybe hope is the door of depression. How hard it is not to put wings on everything. *Evening, window, soul*.

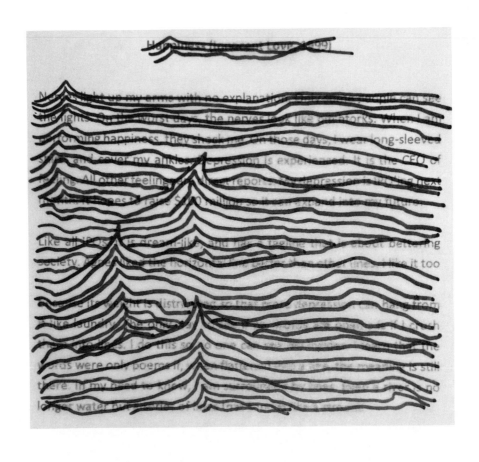

Happiness (from Innocent Love Series, 1999)

Nerves light up my arms with no explanation. Only some people can see the lights. On the worst days, the nerves look like pitchforks. When I am performing happiness, they shock me. On those days, I wear long-sleeved shirts and cover my ankles. Depression is experienced. It is the CEO of feeling. All other feelings are direct reports. My depression is IPOing next month. It hopes to raise $100 million so it can expand into my future.

Like all IPOs, it is dreamlike and has a tagline that is about bettering society. Agnes liked the horizontal line better than other lines. I like it too

because its weight is distributed so that more depression can hang from it like laundry. The only way to see if my words are poems is if I crush them into lines. I do this so no one can see my insides. I've learned that the words are only poems if, when flattened into a line, the meaning is still there. In my need to know, I am surrounded by lines. Even a river is no longer water but a series of lines that sounds like a stream.

Untitled #1, 2003

The two black triangles look like murderers. I realize they and their yellow tips are distractions. They block two horizontal lines underneath. I brush my long black hair vertically. Depression is vertical, always easy to brush through, knotless, silky. No one ever witnesses me brushing it. Even a shadow has a witness, the body. If something is within view but not looked at, is it still being witnessed? A woman spends an hour blow-drying my hair every 12 weeks. She trims off the ends, the parts that keep reaching for happiness. On the floor, they finally look happy in their solitude. I look at Agnes's black triangles for the third time today. This time, I see secret brushstrokes at the top of the canvas. And the reverse gray triangle in the middle. Sometimes I hold a secret in my body for so long that it begins to resemble my cells. Depression isn't actually the secret, but has a secret. I gave up trying to locate depression's antecedent. When we don't know where something comes from, it belongs to no one and is free.

Homage to Life, 2003

This black trapezoid isn't named death or murder or what a lover promises in the dark. Agnes named it *Homage to Life*. Near the end of her life, Agnes lived in an assisted living facility. Everything violent in the world can be made beautiful with language. Someone *passes*, *departs*, or *succumbs*. This is called *advertising*. The grids are finally gone. Even while at the facility, Agnes drove to her art studio each day to work. I think about the people who bathed her, who cut up her food into trapezoids. I wonder when she stopped painting and if she knew. I have a feeling the shape of her last breath was no longer a rectangle. I have a feeling her last word was in the shape of sovereignty. Every poem is trying to be the last free words on earth.

Leaf in the Wind, 1963

Yesterday I slung my depression on my back and went to the museum. I only asked four attendants where the Agnes painting was and the fifth one knew. I walked into the room and saw it right away. From afar, it was a large white square. I thought of my childhood home, white-washed siding and the door my mother painted red so we would not vanish. This was not that house. As I got closer, I could see the pencil lines. In the middle of the painting, a blotch of white. I thought all day about the extra paint. It was so hot that I forgot to read my depression into everything. That day, I brought a daughter with me. We spent the day so close to each other's unhappiness that they began to smear together into a new form. Seven months later, I have cut eight lines off of this poem for no other reason except that they were lies. Perhaps all lines are lies.

Play, 1966

In 27 days, my depression has reorganized into grids. I now know that my heart is made of 1,376 grids. Trying to pull the rectangles together is no longer the objective. I used to make parts into wholes, force snowfall into lines. Is it possible to write down how we feel without betraying our feelings? Once I write the word *depression*, it is no longer my feeling. It is now on view for others to walk toward, lean in, and peer at. I have stared at this painting all morning and wondered whether it's gray or white, both, or neither. Whether the lines are really there or if they are the beginning of my leaving. Pessoa once wrote, *a real and true unity/Is a disease of our ideas*. Maybe we are small pieces without a whole, and there is no one self, just the old selves alongside the newer selves, and looking for a whole is depression. Which is why my depression on view isn't actually on a canvas at all but it is in the air and illegible.

Grey Stone II, 1961

I buy tears at the store for $11.99. When I tilt my head back to drop them in, I see the bottom of God's shoes. I'm surprised by how dirty and used they are. Lately I see them pacing above me more and more. I can't tell if God is here to get me, help me, or scold me. Agnes used a pencil to score her painting, as if to fix something. Very few things never need surgery. The sky, rain, the word *happy*. I hold so tightly on to my pencil that I take it to sleep with me. On some days, I see a flash of light from my hand and fear it is happiness. I wave my hand wildly into the wind until the yellow pencil reappears. Yesterday, after seeing an Agnes painting in person, I decided to cut off my hand to save the pencil. It turns out my blood is white, the texture of gesso, and the pencil wasn't the one that needed saving. What happens when you're not supposed to be depressed? When depression becomes the form of your happiness? When your happiness is so sure of itself that it leaves only its form behind?

The Beach, 1964

The Beach, 1964

If I hold up my hand to a light, I can see the veins in my fingers. The pumping force of the heart should have told us that life is a struggle in one direction, and the letdown of an endless loop, as we wait for the loop to be cut like a ribbon. There are just two epiphanies in life, one is beauty, two is death. What I have learned is that if I wait long enough, every other feeling will disappear. Except for grief. The heart is just one bonfire. From space, it's hard to tell which fire just died out. Agnes's friend Ad Reinhardt died at 53 years old of a heart attack. In his final years, he painted a series of black canvases called his *ultimate paintings*. I think he meant *best* not *last*, but sometimes words get confused. The phone itself never actually *dies*. The heart does stop but the love remains until the last person who holds a memory dies. So everyone dies more than once. I imagine Agnes drawing each line across the canvas and am relieved the photo is too small for me to count the lines. To know that we can, is the conundrum. That we can die or have a different life. That the act of closing our eyes can mean trying not to see or trying to see. That we can cut the canvas in half and burn it in a bonfire or paint it all black, without realizing we've made our own coffin.

Flower in the Wind, 1963

The flower in the wind can only move as much as the wind allows it to move. In this way, it is unmoored while moored. Have you ever been escorted by a man into a room? The way his hand pushes the door open, how he gently puts his hand on your back. And because your back is to him, the touch feels both like comfort and a sudden blade. When the coroner cuts me open, light will spill out onto the metal table, then onto the floor. The light will be discolored by the ambition of men. At the very back of a woman's body is a large shield. We were meant to use it daily but sometimes the pull of the men was too much. This is why the shield can be passed on. None of us use it the way it was meant to be used. It's hard to know what men want from us but a chance to strike their sword on a shield made of light. And when the woman finally gives him some light, he can pull the dripping sword out of her back. *So many people would die to have what you have,* a man said to me yesterday. I told him that the conundrum is there, in the sentence.

Wheat, 1957

I waited three months to see the wheat. When I finally entered the small heptagon that they had built for Agnes's paintings, it was the wrong shape. The paintings were too close together so that the grays, blues, and whites began to blend

like childhood, but the other childhood, the one written over by memory. In Agnes's room, I tried to remember my childhood wonder but couldn't. Just gallows, labyrinths, blood. But now, many days later, I look at my photo of

into each other. On the plane back, I had an aisle seat, but I could still see the sun's pink horizontal strip from Agnes's painting, and I felt that everything wrong with the world was vertical. The way the sun spread itself was like Agnes's line, familiar

Agnes's wheat and think of my mistake—that wonder is in objects not memories. This entire time, I have been slaughtered by memories. In front of me, all along, the dandelion, the petoskey, the ring.

Untitled #5, 1998

In the Cy Twombly room, I wanted so badly to be drawn on. The
curves of Twombly's crayon as if possessed by syntax. Each tiny

white curve on the canvas, a choke hold. That day I was small, as if
I knew I was made by mistake. I walked from Twombly's room to

Agnes's room without flinching. How easy to move from curves to
lines when I used my legs, not my mind. Perhaps every person

has many rooms. We can be divided into 9 sections of 11 lines. Each
line is something seen for the first time. Maybe every poem is an

attempt to describe lightning. Maybe lightning can't be described
which is why there are so many poems. It seems that we are all

doing the same thing, opening our mouths and scribbling. Because
it is all we can do. We are mere trespassers. We inherit nothing but

a body with a mouth and a hand. Some of us spend our lives trying
to pin language to the sky but language is the one that gets to stay.

Sometimes I think about the child that the grandfather dropped out
the window of the ship, and wonder what happened

to the scream that went down the side of the boat. And where all
the people who heard it went.

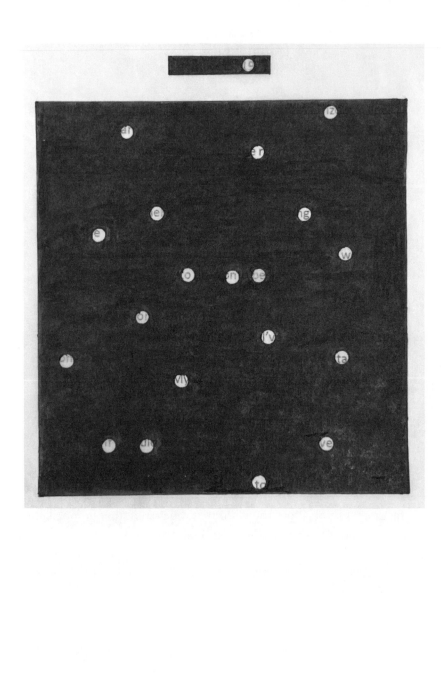

Untitled #5, 1977

I count 36 rectangles, eight vertical and three horizontal lines. As I lean in, I can see the brushstrokes which also look like lines. We are talking to each other across the room but every sentence ends in a field. I forgive Agnes for giving us everything and

nothing. I betray her brushstrokes by looking at the lines. I betray the lines by looking at the brushstrokes. Still, we talked and I began to see our words in the painting. Two poets searching for something to hold on to besides a moon that has

sold out to everyone. Lately I have spent my nights with my ax trying to take down the moon's glow. I've lost my faith in the moon. The way it waits for us to see it. The way it stares at us until we write about it. My work isn't soundless, though. It's

more like the sound of my sleeve catching fire, nothing like what I expected. If I would have known this, I would have used a gun instead. The worst part of desire is the way the moon shines on you for all to see, while you are trying to hack it into pieces.

Drift of Summer, 1965

Summer is already over but it is still here, in each rectangle. If I lean in, I can hear the scratch of the graphite on the canvas. I wonder if Agnes knew that 56 years later we would be in this room, so close to her painting that we could see that each rectangle isn't empty, but contains four lines. Joan Mitchell only titled her paintings when asked. Then maybe this one isn't really about summer, but about how suffering quadruples if you look at it too closely. Or maybe how not everything needs to be about our suffering and how we overcame it. Or how things can be divided again and again and still be beautiful to look at. Or how the interval between today and now really does shorten as we age.

Night Sea, 1963

In this room, my loneliness doubles because the edges of the painting are no longer white. The real blue looks thicker than in the photos. The source of the blue is no longer here. What's left, just the thick beauty in front of me, the frayed edges like my filthy mouth for all to see. I still have my soul, but parts of it have begun to migrate onto beautiful things, like this blue. I leave some of my soul here, three lines up, fourth rectangle over from the right. My soul is made of words and cut glass. Lately, the glass keeps cutting the words. The most wounded words I've had since childhood choose to stay here. I console myself as I exit the room. The people in the room are unaware of what I've done. Some of my words have changed their minds and are trying to leave the room and follow me. I walk away, lighter, a smaller soul on my back. But thirty-three days later, I can still hear them begging.

Untitled #9, 1981

I passed by this painting too quickly. Its colorful bands
of red, blue, and white. A group of 18 bands on top and
another on the bottom. Agnes left the middle empty, but
only now can I see the pencil grids. The painting parts like
a mouth about to say something, but the net of grids holds
everything back. I remember rushing to the blue painting
because this one seemed too happy. I only

remember the stairs at the museum that day. The way they
pitched the September 18 light and made me look divided.
And the way I went ahead of everyone so my day with
Agnes wouldn't end. I never wanted this painting. I used it
to be able to walk past something rapturous toward some-
thing lonely. Now I think they are the same thing. I am
startled to see that it is still September 18 now.

Untitled #9, 1995

Agnes only had nine years to live. The angels must have begun to hover around her canvas like monkeys. This canvas has nine white thin strips between the red and blue ones. I've spent my life thinking about the blue ones, thinking they were the future. But the future was red all along. I sense something is ending but I'm not sure what. Maybe it's the future. This morning, I looked at a large spiderweb above my car. When I returned 10 minutes later, the weaver was gone, the web dismantled, but my hands were still open. Maybe a life doesn't matter so much as the feeling it leaves behind, whether anyone receives the feeling or not. Maybe our goal is to spend all the light. Since none of us asked to be born.

Friendship, 1963

I came to the city so I could see gold. When I arrived though, the leaves were gold too and I became confused. I called the front desk four times and Angel answered each time. By the third call, he ended with *talk soon*. In the morning, a different man answered and I burst into tears. On 53rd Street, small children kept on running into me. A father yelled so loudly at the boy on the scooter that I thought he knew I was carrying death on my back. By the time I arrived at the museum, there was a long line. The bald man in front of me kept turning around to look at me. I could tell by his forehead that he could hurt me. When I finally found the room, I was the only one in there. Everyone else was below me, in the Picasso room. While I stared at the gold rectangles, two attendants talked about whether to work overtime and get paid time and a half. I wanted to tell them that there's no such thing as time, just time and a half. Sometime in the night, Etel Adnan had died. I had just seen her paintings the day before. The crowds were large and I wondered whether our looking had accelerated her death. When I took a photo of Agnes's piece, I saw my dark reflection on the gold. I started counting the grids but the bald man came up next to me. Suddenly there were two dark shadows on the gold. I asked him to step away but when he said, *No*, it was Agnes's voice.

Notes and Sources

The title of this book is borrowed from Agnes Martin's painting of the same title. The titles of the poems are exact titles of Agnes Martin's artwork.

Throughout the book, I refer to Agnes Martin as "Agnes," not out of disrespect or presumption of intimacy and familiarity, particularly in contrast to how I refer to other artists by their surnames. Rather, I was aware of my use of Martin's first name and decided to keep the address the way I had it when I originally drafted the poems because the gesture felt important to the process of making and I wanted to maintain that process in the poems as much as possible.

Lynne Cooke, Karen Kelly, and Barbara Shröder, editors, *Agnes Martin: Essays*, Dia Art Foundation and Yale University Press, 2011.

Frances Morris and Tiffany Bell, editors, *Agnes Martin*, Distributed Art Publishers, 2015.

Nancy Princenthal, *Agnes Martin: Her Life and Art*, Thames & Hudson, 2015.

In "With My Back to the World, 1997," a line references and responds to R.S. Thomas's poem "Senior," in which he writes: "Is there a / sentence without words?" from *Collected Poems, 1945–1990*, Phoenix (U.K.), 1993.

"On a Clear Day, 1973" is a poem that was commissioned by the Museum of Modern Art. The poem references the Atlanta shootings in which Robert Aaron Long killed eight people, of whom six were Asian American women. This commission sparked the other poems in this book.

In "Summer, 1964," Mary Ruefle's "cryalog" is from her essay on menopause, "Pause," from *My Private Property* (Wave Books, 2017). "Little Sister" references this essay too.

In "The Islands, 1961," Pessoa's line is from *The Complete Works of Alberto Caeiro* (New Directions, 2020).

In "Today," Rilke's line is from the First Duino Elegy, *The Selected Poetry of Rainer Maria Rilke*, translated by Stephen Mitchell (Vintage, 1989).

"Today" is written in ten-syllable lines. "Poets are useless" is from H.D.'s *Trilogy* (New Directions, 1998). Etel Adnan's line is from *Time*, translated by Sarah Riggs (Nightboat Books, 2019).

In "Untitled #5, 1998," Stéphane Mallarmé's quote is from a letter Mallarmé wrote to Henri Cazalis in 1864.

Acknowledgments

Thank you to the editors of the following journals, in which many of the poems in this book appeared, sometimes in earlier forms:

Academy of American Poets *Poem-a-Day*: "Grass, 1967"

AGNI: "Perfect Happiness (from Innocent Love Series, 1999)," "Happiness (from Innocent Love Series, 1999)," and "Untitled #12, 1981"

The American Poetry Review: "Gratitude, 2001," "Untitled #5, 1998," "Untitled #9, 1981," "Friendship, 1963," and "The Beach, 1964"

The Atlantic: "Friendship, 1963" and "On a Clear Day"

Guernica: "Untitled IX, 1982"

Harvard Review: "Aspiration, 1960" and "Drift of Summer, 1964"

High Country News: "Untitled #5, 1998"

Image: "The Islands, 1961" and "Homage to Life, 2003"

The Kenyon Review: "Mountain, 1960," "Untitled #10, 2002," "Leaf in the Wind, 1963," "Flower in the Wind, 1963," and "Wheat, 1957"

MoMA magazine and website: "On a Clear Day, 1973"

The New England Review: "Happy Holiday, 1999"

The New Yorker: "Night Sea, 1963"

The Oxonian Review: "With My Back to the World, 1997," "Song, 1962," "Untitled #3, 1994," "Little Sister," and "Untitled, 1960" ("Agnes incised her grids onto the wet blue wound . . .")

The Paris Review: "Red Bird, 1964" and "Innocent Love (from Innocent Love Series, 1999)"

Ploughshares: "The Tree, 1964"

Poetry: "Untitled #9, 1995," "Untitled, 2004," "Starlight, 1962," and "Today"

Poetry London: "Untitled #1, 2003"

Provincetown Arts: "Leaves, 1966," "Untitled #5, 1977," and "Untitled, 1961"

A Public Space: "Buds, 1959"

32 Poems: "Fiesta, 1985"

The Yale Review: "Summer, 1964" and "Untitled, 1978"

Thank you to the Ucross Foundation for granting me an Artist Residency Fellowship in February 2022, where the middle poem, "Today," was written. I also made some of the illustrations while there.

Thank you to the Chowdhury Prize in Literature, the Subir and Malini Chowdhury Foundation, USC, Kenyon College, and *The Kenyon Review* for the encouragement and support.

Thank you to all my friends and supporters. Special thanks go to Mitzi Angel, Sarah Castleton, Sarah Chalfant, Jacqueline Ko, and Kristi Murray for believing in the work and me. Thanks always to my family, and my late mother and father. And thank you to Agnes Martin and On Kawara for the inspiration.